ABOUT THE AUTHOR

Ellen McAteer, a poet and songwriter, is the founder of tell it slant poetry bookshop in Glasgow, and Publishing Manager of the Poetry Translation Centre, and has also worked with Poetry London and the Poetry Society. Their poetry pamphlet *Honesty Mirror* won the New Writer Magazine prize, and is published by Red Squirrel Press. Their first full collection, *My Deep and Gorgeous Thirst*, is published by VERVE Poetry Press. They are one of the London Library Emerging Writers cohort for 2023-24. They won a Waterstones Poetry Competition, and have been shortlisted for the Baker Prize and the Bridport Prize, and long listed for the National Poetry Competition. Their song Blue Valentine won a BBC radio competition, and has been used in a TV advert. They have been a visiting lecturer the Glasgow School of Art and the University of Oxford, a mentee of the Clydebuilt Verse Apprenticeship Scheme, with Alexander Hutchison, and a singer with the band Stone Tape. They received an Arts Council England grant to develop their creative practice in 2020, which included mentorship by Rachel Long.

ABOUT *My Deep and Gorgeous Thirst*

'This is a journey of a collection exploring the rugged terrain of the heart; of family, fragmented place, memory, dialect, class.'
Rachel Long

'With seeming ease and without artifice Ellen McAteer builds strong, fiercely unsentimental poems with surprising serendipities. *In My Deep and Gorgeous Thirst*, McAteer explores the place of place and the place of her people through a sadness tempered with anger, coming to ownership with a clear acceptance, a profound humanity. A slant, powerful, insightful debut.' **Gerry Loose**

'These are poems that contain all the blood and guts and love and pain of family. Poems that take you deep into places that you have never been but which you nevertheless know intimately. Poems that you want to sing along to. Poems that you want to drink along to. Poems that are at once comforting and troubling. Some of the poems here are so beautifully crafted that you feel sure they must be the work of decades, and others feel surely like they must have arrived all at once in a lightning bolt. There is so much to enjoy in this book by Ellen McAteer.'
Henry Bell

'From the psychological and physical horrors of a hospital emergency ward "When the metal folding cot eats my brother, and he screams as it bites, I try to bewitch it open"; to the fanning out *My Deep and Gorgeous Thirst* — Ellen McAteer bewitches us, and yet does not shy away from hard subjects; ones she confronts with an intricate lace of words, with the skill of a surgeon's scalpel. She writes, "In a desperate desire to escape the white room, I feel the wriggle inside me, a swallowed spider of awkwardness force-fed to me by the teacher to catch a fly which was swallowed because it wanted to disappear." McAteer's poetry is simultaneously visceral, playful and colourful, one that "reveal our stark truth". Using free verse and prose poetry modes, she injects an energy into her lines that make them leap out of the page. "Molest me with your tongue instead", she says, urging us to read her work, rewarding us with "the mirror's cold unblinking gaze." This book demands reading and rereading.' **Sudeep Sen**

My Deep and Gorgeous Thirst

Ellen McAteer

VERVE
POETRY PRESS
BIRMINGHAM

PUBLISHED BY VERVE POETRY PRESS
https://vervepoetrypress.com
mail@vervepoetrypress.com

All rights reserved
© 2024 Ellen McAteer

The right of Ellen McAteer to be identified as author of this work has been asserted in accordance with section 77 of the Copyright, Designs and Patents Act 1988.

No part of this work may be reproduced, stored or transmitted in any form or by any means, graphic, electronic, recorded or mechanical, without the prior written permission of the publisher.

FIRST PUBLISHED OCT 2024

Printed and bound in the UK
by ImprintDigital, Exeter

ISBN: 978-1-913917-57-9

Cover photograph: Amy Rafferty

*Dedicated in loving memory to Gerry Loose,
poet, lifelong mentor, and friend.*

'such a small beetle passes so
easily across the written lines I labour over'

*- from Gerry's poem 'The Deer Path To My Door'
(in* Printed on Water, Shearsman, 2007*)*

CONTENTS

Accidentals

Emergency	11
Impact	12
Trauma Fracture	13
My Name is Carnival	14
Buried Alive	15
I Know an Old Woman	16
Missing Child	17
Mother's Day	18
Sophia Loren Plays me in a Movie	19
Doctor Jazz	20

Drouth

The Best Bar in the World	23
My Deep and Gorgeous Thirst	24
My Mother as Snake	26
The Dead Go Barefoot	27
Selkie Wife	28
Ballad of the Fallen	29
Women's Group, Pier Road Drug and Alcohol Project	30
While Bleeding	31
Drouth	32

Psychogeography

Mourning in Arduaine	35
Shoveling Bones	36
Edgeland	37
Hefted	38
On Cnoc Fola (Bloody Foreland)	40
Stormbringer	41
Shattered	42
The North Wind's Reply	43

Yonic

The Big Bad	45
Hiding in Plain Sight	46
Digging the Seaside Goth	48
Urban Ravens	49
A Green Rose	50
Portrait in a Cracked Mirror	51
Gorgon	52
Vampire	53
Not Mad, Just Built That Way	54
The Engineer	55
Birth Trauma Psychosis	56
Pause	57

Acknowledgements

My Deep and Gorgeous Thirst

Accidentals

Emergency

When the metal folding cot eats my brother, and he screams as it bites, I try to bewitch it open – *if I were magic, I would magic that* – I forget the spell, and cry out for my mother, but she doesn't come.

When the white ambulance swallows him and me and, screaming blue murder, vanishes like a pill down the throat of a tunnel, I believe that our disappeared mother must be dead not to fly after it with coat flapping black and feathered, the purple silk oiled like a seabird's underwing.

When, finally, she walks into the hospital, clutching a red balloon, smiling tight, my own throat restricts as I swallow my medicine, paintings of rainbows lying to my face.

Impact

Sky blue as a medical glove. The car crests a verdigris quilt of hills, sun breaks on eggshell waves. A child in the back seat, safe, safe. It was a new time

until we crashed into that wall, took the corner off it, with me halfway out the passenger seat. I must not forget

that family is only as safe as a jigsaw when the box is shaken. Mum's head badly jammed onto the body of my sister, who drove off with me halfway out the door.

My mother once floored the accelerator just so, when I tried to get out of her car during a disagreement. She shouted just so, when I got between my sister and the hairbrush cracking down towards her back.

I don't remember the holiday at all. Day doesn't mean more light. Glove yourself in drink like two blue hands. Never touch this memory with bare skin.

Trauma Fracture

A motorway slip road pile of smashed vehicles clean as a climbing frame and brightly coloured, no hair clinging to a scrap of bone on the steering wheel, no crisp meat, only tiny galaxies of broken glass spiraling on the pavement with a child in blue laughing and running through it surrounded by suitcases vomiting clothes.

Why is he laughing, doesn't he know it's not safe to run out on the road, between angry people armoured in metal running with oil and blood? My brother ran out into traffic once

and the bang was like a door slamming. He flew as he had always wanted to, and I promised a god my father had already killed that I would read his book if he saved my brother.

My son likes to step on cracks, frozen in the middle of the tarmac black and buckled like waves in a photograph. Like a film trick, white lines pricking the eye.

My Name is Carnival

'I read your words like black hungry birds read every sowing.'
Jackson C. Frank

Since I was a skinny   toddling scrap   of fuchsia frock I
hid   from gunmetal eyes   and hard hands, and   read
as soon as   I was able, glad to   skedaddle from   your
need for loud   parading sideshow smiles   with words
between bookcovers   that opened trapdoor into worlds like
blessed secret   doors on a stage set   safe and warm   black
sub rosa dens   where I fed   blood tales   to   hungry
baby siblings   out of my own maw   just as mama birds
regorge   crop milk   to flamingo hatchlings   I   read
to them as   they bent under   my wing   they rode every
storm out   in watery creches   gobbling stories I was sowing.

Buried Alive

Walking the threadbare machair with my brother, the blue stone road unspooling to the tangled sea, rabbit holes dark against the gold-grassed dunes, wildflowers patterning the green, I remind him of the time we found the whole skeleton of a horse in the bog nearby. All we found was a jawbone, but now he remembers it just as I told it: the day we saw a whole horse in the wet peat, bones white as chair legs, sucked alive into the bog.

When he was little, I made him run home with: 'Look how the clouds seem to be being posted through a giant letterbox over the sea.' He ran screaming from the picture my words made. I discovered witch-craft that day. The jawbone we carried home to our museum of interesting things. The maggots that pushed the teeth from his jaw. The silver lawn of mould on a softening jack-o-lantern. Halloween chocolates turning white. Black flies hatching in his rabbit-riddled mind.

I Know an Old Woman

In a desperate desire to escape the white room, I feel the wriggle inside me, a swallowed spider of awkwardness force-fed to me by the teacher to catch a fly which was swallowed because it wanted to disappear. I did not expect the teacher to take a spider out of a box and ram it down my throat till the only escape from the pain and discomfort is staring out a window at anything far away. Father chimney, big mother dome, the horizon always blurred, the unknown a comfort as against having something black and wriggling shoved between your lips, like being forced to swallow a page you wrote, to fish up the feeling hidden behind it.

It is a fisting level of violation. Not the spider but the fly is being hunted, green and bright, before it lays its eggs in secret. If not swallowed that fly would bash against the window pane eventually, as my mind does, buzzing and thumping angrily trying to get at the light beyond the pane, the air, while the spider crawls back up out of my mouth after it, pulls it back inside again, bound in its web, a big, furry grey pill for me to swallow. It kills me dead, of course, of course.

Missing Child

Mornings I shot out of the window of our basement flat, unfolding through the bars like a cat sleek with pale fur, and lay in the filthy wet grass. My brother and I drew worlds on the pavement, adventured every crack and root bump. No-one told me I was a girl, or even human. We roamed the hills. Everything was bright green and blue. Mirrors were as irrelevant as the dark fringed ponds that we weren't allowed to go beyond.

We moved to the city and glass ground itself into my knee. Kids in white trainers barked at our old patched clothes; laughed at my red coat. Mum told me not to tuck my t-shirt into my jeans. The mothers of my brother's friends told me not to climb trees, shouted me down from the scaffolding, called me dirty. Asked why I was playing with their sons. Their tension infected the boys, who started to stare, to pounce, to pull hair.

I sat loose-clothed on a bench alone. A man came and asked me to play. I ran to my friend's window, hammered till their mother let me in. She called the police, *no wonder, running wild*. My tomboy self got into his car that day, was left a flat hard body folded into a bin-bag by the road, pink and blue chalk dust on their fingers, broken glass buried in their knees.

Mother's Day

Barnacle babies. Tiny toads grown into handsome princes. They still suckle the life out of me. I feel like depleted soil, swollen with rain and washed away. A fungal root system growing in my whispering insides, mycorrhiza in my rhizosphere. My ovaries, once balanced as a set of scales, producing babies in fat clusters, now not even good enough for wine, red bands binding my birth control to the wall. What homunculi would these old vines drop now? Tiny black-furred fledgling chicks, red-beaked, hungry. Vampire babies. But mothers are scales. They must suffer tidily, everything very well put away. Made mother by my man. He feeds me till I become my mother-in-law. Suckles at my breast. Tries to climb inside. My loinfruit bring me pink roses, a cluster on a vine. Bath salts, pink pink pink. They want to cleanse me. Virginise me. Bury me. Like a bonewhite sacrifice.

Sophia Loren Plays me in a Movie

A flag the colour of dried blood hangs from the railings of the courtyard. A second flag, emptied like water over the opposite rail, is smoothed like a sheet by a female hand while a capped man empties his paper bags of rubbish. Uniforms start flowing like a monochrome river under the waterfall flag.

A music of bells and wheels fades to an alarm clock loud inside a house. A caged bird whistles its own alarm. Dimples of disappointment blooming around her mouth, her breasts heavy under a ragdoll apron, a weatherworn statue of a goddess, ironing at 5am, sugars hot coffee, gathers clean clothes, and starts the dance of waking the household, child by child, bringing a half-drunk cup to her husband.

For all she knows, men working and children going to school were invented by women for a bit of peace, but the joke is on us, she thinks, one mum to every family? This family needs three. One to do laundry, one to wash up and cook, and one to stay in bed all day. The bird taunts her with the wrong name, calls for its breakfast, and escapes its cage.

Her eyes have wings. They follow the bird across the courtyard. Both watch two men dancing in the apartment opposite. A loud, official knock interrupts the music.

'Mama, only for you my song flies. Mama, long as I'm here you'll never be alone...'

Doctor Jazz

Keys, I have a whole tinful, to houses I won't see again. Out back was a wilderness, trees and the pub and don't go beyond the road or the river. *Hello central, get me Doctor Jazz. He's got just what I need, I'll say he has.*

A greenbrown edgeland paradise. Freedom that could be watched. Boarded up houses safer than the street, though we walked beams for non-existent rooves. Coins of green and gold falling from the trees. There is flesh, pink, brown, smooth, warm and oiled. There is tobacco in the air, scraps of dried leaves on the tongue, the yeastbright smell of happy adults, daisies in the mud which means safe, the sound of the record player, a child who does not fear the hairbrush on the back today. *When the world goes wrong and I've got the blues, he's the guy who makes me put on both my dancin' shoes.*

If I can be a background tune, a daub in a sketchbook, the painting will not turn blue and mottled white, it will stay green and gold, the grownups brimming with beer, sweet ruby wine, yellow-edged fingers in Golden Virginia, rub and roll, watch soft smoke flow, while Jellyroll Morton sings: *The more I get, the more I want it seems. I see Doctor Jazz in all my dreams.*

Drouth

The Best Bar in the World

was an old air raid shelter
up a rural winter alley.

Cans of Stella under the stars
coffee in the morning mist
while the swallows swam the cold
upstream and the train
took flocks of commuters
up the line. After the false dawn

of the TV screen, the window is
a tall white drink of light.
The postman wears a halo.
The bus shelter fills with gold,
spills it onto the platform as a wave
of gulls catches the light on a turn.

Leaves hold a brighter green to the silver
of this waking. Salt sparkles on the path
but the ground is too warm for frost, blue
flowers surprising the eye between the feet.

Tell me, would I see this glory if other people
had not worn me down to this, a brown leaf
spinning in the busy wind, a veined dry thing
not registered by passing eyes?

My Deep and Gorgeous Thirst

It started in the throat of my grandfather,
riding boxcars in the dustbowl thirties,
dreaming big rock candy mountains,
little streams of alcohol a-trickling.
Shipbuilding in Glasgow, wartime,
pubs that opened before dawn to
dull the drouth of the nightshift.

It sang from the throat of my grandmother
Irish come-all-ye's, craic with Rosie mór,
feywild tales, ghosts and playing cards,
her jealous husband spitting in the fire,
banshee sheep crying like children,
beaten children greetin' for
a wee bawbee she never had.

It mumbled from the smothered mouth
of my mother's mother, pilot's widow,
honeymoon crashed with the plane,
child actress become child bride to
an old man who could keep her.
He stopped her playing piano,
sent the kid away to school.

It rang through the hungry, damaged body
of my mother, whom they called 'Chai'
not child, in boarding school at three,
forbidden to sing, mouthing words,
carving her anger on the walls
till the nuns, in pity, fed her,
which taught her protest.

It prickled within my thin-skinned father,
whipped raw by the don'ts of a priest
who took a grim-mouthed pleasure
in describing sins that the bairn
could never have imagined.
Which taught him to wrap
himself in drink and song.

Tumbling down all those dry throats
into me, spirit sharpens the gimlet
in my burned mouth. I am under
the slow cold river looking up,
bloated like a trapped corpse,
drunk, and by drunk I mean
swallied, fou, drowned.

My Mother as Snake

Her hair cropped
cancer close and
moulting. Her face
white translucence
of empty scales -
clear and puckered.
Bare feet shucked
cold, blue, devoid
of blood. Only her
eyes still bright
as she wriggles
the skin of life
almost off her.

The Dead Go Barefoot

It'll have to be Shanks's Pony,
my father's ghost remarks in passing,
as I walk the London woods,
carrying my anger as he did,
Limping as he took the miles
on a shattered toe unnoticed
till it fused and broke his stride.
It will have to be rebroken
the doctor said, but no.
Drinking to dull the ache,
he chose to keep on walking.

Selkie Wife

I weave a skin from hedge-gin
to cover the raw meat of my face
exposed by my husband's theft.
He watched me from the edge.
of the party. In the dark hall,
he found and hid my hide from me.
I know it is in this house. I hear it
humming from one of the boxes
buried in the roof's crawl-space.
I hear my sons singing too,
whispering to the waves' beat.
Their music is subtler than mine,
bitter and sharp-toothed, leave me
a chewed bloody steak on a plate.
I don't sing any more. My guitar
sits gathering dust on the wall.
Closest thing I have to skin, now,
is the leather bindings on this row
of notebooks, recently unpacked,
faded ink wrinkling their pages.

Ballad of the Fallen

What funny animals we are to poison ourselves for fun,
$\qquad\qquad\qquad\qquad\qquad\qquad\qquad\qquad$ said my son.
Yesterday I drank till I bled with a friend who is the horn
to my horn in the Charlie Haden *Silence*   G
two b-flat trumpets on cocaine   Db
we blow together over glasses   Cm
brimful of the hateful stuff   Ebm

...and yet I love this poison
   cold and clear as a teardrop
though I wear the names
of every friend it killed
inked and scarred.
My lantern lady.
Her great heart
froze under
its cold
clear
gaze
not
waking her husband beside her.

Women's Group, Pier Road Drug and Alcohol Project

We are like hooded crows tied to a hedge,
limp-bodied, grey-feathered.

Our beaks open, crying loud at first,
then gaping silent.

We cannot name it, the thing that binds.
All we know is

when we open our wings, we are bitten
by sharp stones.

We can hear the hungry calling of our
hatchlings, out of reach.

All the farmer knows is to string us along
the fence as a warning.

While Bleeding

out at the crack of noon
I wear perfume to mask the tang
of metal in the air around me;
the smell of my moon river.
A crow nods on a bin bag
gutting and gobbling.
I feel a dry pinch
witch fingers stirring.
Branches ink the sky.
I wear my father's hat
it lines my face in black
I walk the ache out
tramping through galleries;
market stalls bloom
bookshelves are ladders
on this leaking ship.
I wait out the call of the cold
glorious icewashed martini;
London gin quieting the din
of my chattering wound.

Drouth

Meaning *thirst,* as in *for knowledge,*
dusty books on flyspecked shelves -

my thirst is not for story but shape
pattern in words and meaning like

a painting you can't quite make out
whose colours seem to bury grins.

Music felt in the bones, a song that
abandons you and haunts you as if

you are a house with a flickering face
moving from window to window,

page to page, glass to glass, magic
lantern eyes, flashing flirting fasting,

starving and thinning like a woman
once plump, now cancer-carved.

Meaning *thirst* as in *for the bevvy*,
an emollient poured, shushing, sharp -

my thirst is not dry but wet as a
rain-slicked road under bald bike tyres,

raw like meat peeled off the bone,
a bitten lip in need of a tongue.

Without the bottle I am without skin,
eczema-red and irritable; sunburned,

blistering, glistening with fluid sacs,
a body in a too-hot bath. A crayfish

transparent, near-invisible,
walking the river-bed, snatched

wriggling into a pot of boiling oil,
pinkening painfully as it dies.

Psychogeography

Mourning in Arduaine

A cool mercury light
water pulling sky to sea
that soft grey sympathy
of rain and stone

Shuna, small and jagged
echoed, with variations,
by Luing
Seil a faint fond shadow
embracing them both

each made of the same stone
and not quite fitting
like broken jigsaw pieces
like family

each an island
holding to itself
but part of an archipelago

even when the rain
tears you from the horizon
I know you are there

I can feel the shape of your shores
through the currents that reach mine

Shoveling Bones

'You think you are taking a clean sheet of paper, and it's already covered with signs, illegible, as by a child's hand.'
Rosemary Waldrop

Three in the afternoon, daydreaming, you
feel the magic word *Friday*, and think
of that cold fire on the tongue, you
feel it licking your lips and belly, are
aware of the desert air that is taking
up space in your womb and liver like a
shout. You were doing so well, were clean,
till your son woke you asking why the sheet
was covered in tomato sauce, the lining of
your stomach colouring the bed like paper
scribbled over and over in red ink, and
you are trying to write a new story, but it's
not possible, script has been written already,
here is your carpet, blotting paper covered
with smudges of brown crayon, spattered with
half-made out words, obscured strange signs,
canyons imprinted from other pages, illegible
but stamping and patterning your own story, as
you write, pen slipping into grooves set by
your parents, your plotline a juvenelia garden,
grubbed up, garbled like a child's version
of a faerie tale, written with guided hand.

Edgeland

Where does the frame begin?
A dirty double mattress coloured clay,
an old sink, deep and enamelled, wet.

Shirts drying in the bushes. Wildflowers
in a wine bottle. A school of cider cans
spill across the grass like goldfish.

Fishing lines wait to catch dinner
in a stagnant old dry dock nearby.
The hanger of bright compact disks

on the chainlink fence is gone, boots still
peeping from a box with a smile printed on,
tired from packaging dreams to buy sleep

Hefted

The Irish house is not mine. It never was,
though I dreamed myself into it often.

I'm the only sibling who visits,
and the road to the sea is the same.

It is my sons who walk it with me,
one on my father's legs, short, strong,

like mine, made for heavy loads and roads,
the other has my mother's back, which is

to say he has mine, question-marked,
a shield against eyes and laughter.

The Scottish house is not mine, nor will be,
though I haunt it often, in memories, holidays.

Ownership is bills and disintegration,
but the road to the sea is the same,

the boys who walk it a little taller, one
with my little sister's big blues, the other

with her strawberry blonde hair thatching
my brother's slate horizon-gazing eyes.

The fruit of my mother's garden
is eaten by whiter teeth and shared.

My parents argued over which house
I was born in, of two on the same street,

and all I have is this London pavement
between them for a greasy birth canal,

two identical front doors, the rooms
and halls behind them rented out.

So while Philemy riddles the top field, two lads
walk the machairs with me on those sea roads

hefted, as I am, my twin lambs, to the land
our ancestors first grazed, remembered how?

On Cnoc Fola (Bloody Foreland)

Granite rocks, hard as ancestors,
big as my grandfather used to be,
ground and spun to giant pebbles
by the wild Atlantic. Remember
his big bright quartzite Ulster voice
that grated, ground and crashed
over the screams of moving metal,
the spark and smash of welding.
He became Scottish: James
became *Jimmy, Big Yin, youse.*
In turn, his son learnt to polish
his flint Glaswegian, shine it up
for company, become a troubadour,
ring the stones together softly, for
those who liked their Scots gentle.
Dance for yer Daddy, my little laddie.
His daughter learned from their mocking
to round her sharp London limescale teeth
river her dry Southeastern chalk tongue
to a plummy BBC neutrality, only betrayed
by words like *garridge* and *baastard,*
and *Gawd you saand dead different!*

Stormbringer

In your siblings' steps you find the sea,
between the fist of Ireland's edge
and Scotland's broken bones,
threatening any vessel sailed across.

To climb aboard will only capsize
your brother mast, your sister sail,
so you rain like it's kicking out the tap,
dripping along portholes, cold fingers

fitting cracks, soaking into decks,
unwelcome, chilling. Storm
and whirlpool at them,
hoping they will anchor.

A sad woman with clocks for eyes
watches for a break in her weather.

Shattered

I'm drifting in my carcass
along the A12.

In the seat beside me
reams of shaved skin -

an address book,
leaflets for a jazz
concert at The Cut,

a letter from the NHS
titled 'Posterior Repair',

a photo exhibition
of lighted arrows
being fired into sea,

a brochure for a coveted
converted barn in Beccles,

a tiny knitted duck
staring with the eyes
of my dead grandson.

The North Wind's Reply

(After Lola Ridge)

I love you, contented
hard bare land,
to which I return.

Flinching under my cold,
your flowers bend,
lose their pollen, rise;

your salt waves peel away
from the inane smile of the
beach, back towards me.

Let me blow upon your
forests of pine, tall,
red, rough-bearded.

I will make the snow dance,
tear earth/skin from stone/bone,
caress you like a breath,

a cataract of cloud blown clear
to reveal our stark truth:
we can never be joined.

Yonic

The Big Bad

I have been mourning him
since he was born
heart open

My daughter's heart
is a hot jar
cracking

I cannot mend
his tiny muscle
so instead I stitch

white buttons like fingernails
seed-pearls like budding teeth
to a little cloth cap

He is to be a Pearly King
in death, for he is London

His sisters take turns to hold
their precious doll whose
clockwork is winding down

I am the Grannie in the story
already eaten by the wolf

Hiding in Plain Sight

According to her
my small letters
and scribblings out

mean I don't want
to be seen. She's
right of course.

I wear my grey hair
like a wig in a bad
made-for-TV play.

Clothe myself in fat
to hide my hunger
for the sea's touch.

I copy the speech
of other housewives,
hang washing in a gang.

What am I hiding?
It is a deep down
echo in a dry well.

Few dip a bucket
these days. When
she does she sees

my eyes are blue
my toenails silver.
There is a water spirit

lurking down that well.
Mornings I pick scales
like sequins off my legs.

Digging the Seaside Goth

*'I grow old, I grow old, I shall wear the bottom
of my trousers rolled.'* T.S. Eliot.

Dark curls fall over her face, beautiful, pallid, scarred. I
watch as she bends, brushes sand between which grow
her toes. The cuffs of her faded skinny denims, old

and wet, wrinking round her bonewhite shins. I
smile at the Dr Martens Chelsea boots which grow
in a line on an apron of sand where sea folds old

waves into tinfoil wrinkles. Walk on water: sunlit I
take the road to nowhere, away from her. Shall
I describe the unsilver striping of the black weed, wear

a clear dead jellyfish set in the ridged gold sand? The
beach has a belly jewel. Blooming at the sea bottom,
red plumes of Corallina. Under a black bin lid of

rainclouds, a tidal pool is shining fiery light like my
bad luck, a smashed mirror, crushed into trousers
and reassembled by crowblack clouds, rock n rolled.

.

Urban Ravens

'I'm picking at the world like an angry scab.'
Jackie Leven

At the Castle on Paradise Street I'm
chasing grape with grain, picking
out which boi I want to flicker at.
The trick is to burn golden like the
flame of a lighter, leave the world
just warmer for your absence, like
lighting a cigarette, pass on an
amber glow that doesn't burn angry.
If they've been scorched, kiss the scab.

A Green Rose

Blushing to flesh in the tightly coiled
spiral of waxy petals that are veined
like labia, a yonic flower, prepuce
I want to force open with my tongue.
I hold the stem tight. A strangled leaf
drops into the pages of my notebook
asking to be pressed and dried.
I was this once, thorns true, reaching

to the light. My own stem cut, I slacken,
Fibonacci twists darkening to musky rust.
It smells green, too young to be scented,
this muscular rose. Fisted leaves curl up
strong and erect; slender, holding shape
like a brand-new pocket empty of fingers.

.

Portrait in a Cracked Mirror

My face is a sugar candy skull, reflected
in the dressing table inherited from my mother,
or a death mask of my father, the one who dropped
the mirror, its beveled edge sliding out of the frame,
the silver, wearing off in flakes, makes migraine gaps.
It reflected their rows and their lovemaking.
At her request, he vanished from it, replaced

by a younger man. Friends again, he had only
moved it to paint the room fresh for her.
She cried at the accident, admitting it's a heavy
thing to carry, balanced but unhinged, hard to shift.
My mother said her soul was in that mirror.
She had grown thinner and wiser in its frame.

Gorgon

My cut hair lies around my feet
    chopped   snakes

reflected in Perseus' shield.
    Be headed   shorn

       I no longer turn folk
to stone.   Athena's painted face

seems to Mona Lisa her
      am I adoring the face

        or   its   paint?
   Unmedusa me goddess

I broke my vow once
     you green my skin.

Moss on a stone
which no longer   rolls.

I was born of   sea water
how could I resist   the sea god?

    I birthed Pegasus   and Chrysaor
from the tides of our passion

    Does this require   castration?
Molest me with your tongue instead.

Vampire

Without the mirror of my mother's face
who will I be?

The silver behind the mirror glass stops
my reflection cold.

Sister, you must be my mirror now
or I will vanish.

My milk teeth were drawn out painfully
before their time.

Warm my marble skin with your sun gaze.
Unblue my lips.

The gold flag of hair all down my back
is dyed now.

Mother me, sister, a babe lying frozen
in your arms,

taken, a death photograph, although
it was you who left.

Not Mad, Just Built That Way

Wine flows like blood
I go mad like an onion

being peeled down to the core
becoming raw and greener.

Cut me and I will make you cry
seeping stinging poison.

I raise red rimmed welts
blur your vision.

Keep chopping
the knife will slip

I will drink your blood
to pink my cells.

The Engineer

His body is a machine that dreams
in metal and movement, fire and oil.

Awake, he digs other people's gardens,
turns their beds, repairs their houses.

Things swell and flourish at his touch,
including my body's neglected furnace.

He digs me up, like a shovel in ash,
cracking and reigniting spent fuel.

His love is vegetable, grows slow,
as the poem said. Like flames. Old

friends, he nods to the robin who hops
fearless among the plates on his table,

a welcome guest who often joins us;
another of the many birds he loves

who love him. I am migratory.
Always leaving, always returning.

He feeds the robin and me from his plate,
feeds the crops, feeds the fire, reads me books.

His father's death untethered him, but he showed
more pain to me for the baby blackbird, lying

starved on a path, wings spread in crucifixion.
Nothing could reignite this feathered engine.

Birth Trauma Psychosis

Her tubes hang out red and blue
an electrical board torn off a wall.
Raw, salted, preserved like fish,
the holy spirit pickled in a jar
the invisible mother, face peeled
and pale like an apple, a clean page
for their stamp of birth bureaucracy,
our lady of desiccated waspblown fruit
a clean slate waiting for the angel's rape.
Her postpartum belly walnut-wrinkled.
Breasts swinging pink, production line udders,
her twin balloons tugging at her loosely held strings,
white as moths wet-hatched.

Pause

The mirror's cold unblinking gaze
shows a woman used up, skin puckered,
salt, pepper and cayenne hair,

tarnished skin, rusted in patches,
black scratches around eyes and mouth,
shoulders rounded with fat, dressed

as one would be leaving the house in a fire.
A patchwork cushion tied up in an apron
used to smother a young tomboy long ago.

This, only she knows - he cries inside it still.
Sometimes, when chores are done, she cuts
him out with scissors, lets him play a while.

ACKNOWLEDGEMENTS

'The Best Bar in the World' was first published in *One for the Road: an anthology of Pubs and Poetry* edited by Stuart Maconie and Helen Mort. (Smith Doorstop, 2017) 'My Mother as Snake' was first published in *Poetry London*, issue 100. Autumn 2021. 'Mourning in Arduaine' was first published in *New Writing Scotland 29*, and was then translated into Dutch by Susan Ridder for the magazine *Awater*. 'My Deep and Gorgeous Thirst' is a quote from the film *The Philadelphia Story* (1940), where Cary Grant says of Katherine Hepburn's character 'She never understood my deep and gorgeous thirst!' I would like to acknowledge Philip Barry, the writer of the original 1939 Broadway play, for this title. The poem 'Sophia Loren Plays me in a Movie' makes oblique reference to the film *Una Giornata Paritcolare* (A Special Day) directed by Ettore Scola, 1977. Compagnia Cinematografica / Champion/ Canafox Films. The song quoted at the end is *Mama* by Beniamino Gigli. The lyrics in Doctor Jazz are from the song *Dr Jazz*, written by Joe "King" Oliver in 1926 and recorded by Jelly Roll Morton. Electrola Records, (Single) 1926. I often use song lyrics and titles in my work, so the following songs must also be acknowledged as inspirations: Charlie Haden, *Silence*; Jackie Leven, *Urban Ravens*; Jackson C. Frank, *I Am Carnival*; John and Beverly Martin, *Stormbringer*.

THANKYOUS

I would like to thank Gerry Loose for reminding me I am a poet, Henry Bell and Louise Welsh for outing me as a poet, Ranjana Thapalyal for employing me as a poet, and Alexander (Sandy) Hutchison and Rachel Long for mentorship. Two of those dear mentors, Gerry and Sandy, are dead. I hope they can hear me. I would also like to thank Kaaren Whitney, Beth Soule and Sue Wallace-Shaddad in Suffolk, Maura Dooley, Richard Scott and my wonderful Wednesday group at Goldsmiths, and the King's Poets, London, for helping to shape these poems. Further thanks go to Jim Carruth at Mirrorball and Christie Williamson at the Scottish Writers' Centre and tell it slant, and the London Library staff and fellow writers. Finally, thanks to Jeremy for dream inspiration, and to Mat, Finn and Charlie, for forbearance and support.

ABOUT VERVE POETRY PRESS

Verve Poetry Press is a prize-winning press that focused initially on meeting a local need in Birmingham - a need for the vibrant poetry scene here in Brum to find a way to present itself to the poetry world via publication. Co-founded by Stuart Bartholomew and Amerah Saleh, it now publishes poets from all corners of the UK - poets that speak to the city's varied and energetic qualities and will contribute to its many poetic stories.

Added to this is a colourful pamphlet series, many featuring poets who have performed at our sister festival - and a poetry show series which captures the magic of longer poetry performance pieces by festival alumni such as Polarbear, Suhaiymah Manzoor-Khan and Imogen Stirling.

The press has been voted Most Innovative Publisher at the Saboteur Awards, and has won the Publisher's Award for Poetry Pamphlets at the Michael Marks Awards.

Like the festival, we strive to think about poetry in inclusive ways and embrace the multiplicity of approaches towards this glorious art.

www.vervepoetrypress.com
@VervePoetryPres
mail@vervepoetrypress.com